ELLIS PARKER BUTLER ON THE FINE ART OF WRITING HUMOR

ELLIS PARKER BUTLER ON THE FINE ART OF WRITING HUMOR

ELLIS PARKER BUTLER

WILDSIDE PRESS

ELLIS PARKER BUTLER ON
THE FINE ART OF WRITING

Published in 2009 by Wildside Press.
www.wildsidepress.com

"Are Sidelines Helpful?" originally appeared in *Writer's Year Book and Market Guide* (1931). "Ellis Parker Butler Talks on Humor" originally appeared in *Writer's Digest*, June, 1935 issue. "Ten Rules for Humor" originally appeared in *Photoplay Magazine*, November, 1920 issue. "This Funny Business" originally appeared in *Writer's Digest*, August 1930 issue. "How I Sell My Stories" originally appeared in *Writer's Diegest*, March 1932 issue. "An Author Glares at Editors" originally appeared in *The Bookman*, anonymously, in the April, 1932 issue. [Assumed to be by Butler.]

CONTENTS

ARE SIDELINES HELPFUL?

Will Rogers is an important humorous writer, he also does a vaudeville stunt, acts in the motion pictures, talks over the radio, and has acted on the legitimate stage. Now and then he talks at a banquet for pay. I saw Will Rogers on the vaudeville stage before he had any humorous chatter except four or five words when his lasso did not behave for him. What he said was "Maybe you don't think so, but I did that trick once," and we all laughed.

Chic Sale wrote The Specialist and it had the largest sale of any humorous book ever published, I imagine. He has a vaudeville stunt, acts in reviews and is — or will be — in the movies.

These two men, extremely different in most respects, are real humorists. Both now do daily humor bits for syndicates. They are not writers with sidelines. They are men who, doing something else, discovered in themselves strains of humor, and put some of their humor into written form. Writing, with them, is the sideline.

Irvin S. Cobb gave us his humor from a different point of departure. He wrote humor, then did some lecture work, and at this moment is doing some radio talking. Cobb would say, I am sure, that writing is his profession, and that these other matters are sidelines with him. Robert Benchley is a writer; his vaudeville stunts are sidelines. We have any number of writers now who follow writing as a profession but do some lecturing on the side, or have some other face-to-face, eye-to-eye or mouth-to-microphone sidelines.

The question I am asking is whether sidelines of any sort are helpful to the writer?

The four men I have mentioned have in them natural wells of the sort of comicality we call humor. Will Rogers discovered his almost by chance, Chic Sale developed his intentionally, Irvin Cobb came upon his as a newspaper writer; I haven't the slightest idea how Benchley discovered his, but all four of these men have the natural actor in them. Cobb telling a story is a real comedian; Benchley is another. For all of these men the personal public appearance means increased prestige. Their sidelines are probably helpful. Rogers' and Sale's writings increase their audience; Cobb and Benchley make new admirers whenever they appear personally.

But for every writer who can increase his prestige in this way we have many who can not. The common remark after a humorist has ended a radio talk is "Well, he's not so funny as I thought he would be." There is such a thing as showmanship, and not many of us have it. Mark Twain and Bill Nye had it, but many others don't.

Occasionally, as a means of making easy money, the best writers have tried a sideline for awhile. Thackeray, for instance, made an American lecture tour, as did Dickens, and as are many present day English writers. Mark Twain always lectured, notably when he made his tour around the world after his book-publishing firm failed. But it should be noted that all these men were well-known — famous, indeed — and that many paid money to see them much as they would have paid to see a two-headed calf. The average writer is neither a two-headed calf nor furiously famous nor as amusing as Clemens, Cobb or Benchley when appearing otherwise than in print.

I have myself done lecture work. I was successful enough, I think, for most of my "dates" wanted me to return. My agent gave me all the dates I could fill. I was paid a high price, as prices ran. I gave it up because I found, at the end of a couple of years, that my total income was just about the same as when I remained at home to write. When I lectured I wrote less. When a man lectures he has many long jumps by train, finds himself in uninspiring hotel rooms, must go to teas and accept other hospitalities, and he is in no condition to do his best writing. Often he has time to do none.

Every sideline takes some of the writer's time and energy. A writer's whole capital is his brain, and when his brain is doing one thing it cannot be doing something else. If a man has a certain time for writing — say from 9 A.M. to 1 P.M. — and customarily relaxes in some way after that, it is evident that if he undertakes another form of work in his relaxation hours he will be less fit when he comes to his writing again. His proper work, which is writing, suffers. He must be a giant of energy if this is not to be so, and I believe Cobb and others who can do so many various things well are such giants. They are exceptions; most of us are not.

Writing is, for most of us, an ample job. It is all we can handle, and it is bad for us to look through the fence at the attractive grass in the next pasture and then try to be in both pastures at once. If we try to eat in both pastures at once we do a worse job than if we stuck to one thing and gave it all our attention.

The writer should stick to his writing. I don't like the verb "to specialize" in connection with writing, but I know no word that so nearly expresses what I would advise the writer to do. The fiction writer should write fiction; the historical writer should write history; the humorist should write humor. His theme may demand magazine or book treatment, but whatever the treatment he should not swerve aside to do something that seems at the moment more attractive.

In my opinion, no writer for the press should undertake to write scenarios for movies or radio use. They are separate professions; they require a specially developed technique. Write your story or your book, and if radio wants it let radio do the scenario; if the pictures want it let the producer make the scenario. If you feel you must write a play do not let it interfere with your proper writing. Do it at night or in spare hours; it is better still to let a real dramatist share with you, he doing the actual dramatization. Dramatization is an art in itself; you will be better employed doing your regular writer's work.

A writer becomes a writer when he picks up his pen or seats himself at his typewriter, but becoming an author is a different story — if you will accept my definition of an author for the moment. Let me say that an author is a writer who has created for himself a recognized place in whatever form of literature he has attempted. This need not be the heavyweight position of a Thackeray, a Balzac, a Howells or an Anatole France. It may be the position of an Alice Duer Miller or a Ben Ames Williams or a Corey Ford or any well-recognized writer in any field. He may be a writer of sentiments for Christmas cards. But an Alice Duer Miller should not fiddle with writing sentiments for Christmas cards — and I'll wager she doesn't.

The writer becomes an author — in the above meaning — by doing the work he has chosen to do and excluding other forms of writing from his schedule. Life is very short, a day is gone almost before it has started, a year goes into the past and the most a writer has written cannot be much in quantity. To build himself a position as an author a man must make every day's work a brick in the structure — and it is surprising how soon the accumulating bricks make a recognized wall if a man does keep true to his chosen plan.

It is the accumulating effect of good work consistently done that establishes a writer and makes his fame and income secure. There is nothing good in jumping from one thing to another, trying this and that, dropping a brick here and a brick there. At the end of a year you have nothing built; in fact, your reputation suffers. Not with editors alone, but with life itself and you yourself.

I would like to point out that Mr. Kipling would have gained nothing by knocking off to do an advertising booklet, to write a scenario, to do six radio-play synopses or to go on a lecture tour. Kipling wrote Kipling stuff.

I don't mean to urge any writer to "specialize" to the extent of writing only "pulp magazine" material or only "coated-paper magazine" material, but I would have writers write, at least until they are so famous that they can lecture with the knowledge that people will pay to see — rather than to hear — them. I would urge writers — particularly those who are rather new at the work — to follow one easily recognized road, the road to be of his own choosing. Shaw, for instance, is known worldwide as the social cynic; Barrie is similarly known for his sentimental charm; Wells for his scientific-political bravo; Mencken for his criticism. The humorist who puts forth a solemnity puzzles the audience he has been creating for his humor; the writer of charming love tales tears down his foundations when he indulges in a cynical essay.

Although all this has a direct and recognizable effect on the writer's market, I am not thinking of that as much as I am of the long-trend happiness and satisfaction of the writer. The happy man is he who sees his public coming to recognize him as true to a definite purpose. "Trying something new" is not all it is cracked up to be. Readers, including editors, like to feel that certain men may be trusted to give them certain things. We like the wren to sing and we do not expect or want it to croak. Particularly we do not want a wren that sings most of the time and croaks when we least expect it. We don't want our apple trees to bear apples one season and dried codfish the next. Out in California they can graft trees so that they bear half a dozen different fruits, but all the favor is still for the tree that bears one kind only and makes a good job of it.

A writer should not try to engage in half a dozen professions. A writer should not try to write two or three varieties of literature. There are no sidelines that benefit the writer half as much as they injure him. When you think of Cobb or Benchley or the few very exceptional writers who do try sidelines and who do succeed in them, just look through the magazines and the bookshops and notice how vastly many more writers do not have sidelines. Notice how many of the successful writers are notable for long-trend faithfulness to types of writing they can do best and how completely they leave other types alone. And then — I wish you could — count up the hundreds of men and women who tried to write forty-seven different kinds of things and are now warming bookkeepers' stools or selling ladies' garments.

When a sideline comes creeping up on you and whines like a puppy to be taken under your wing — as it will — take it by the neck and throw it seven miles. Eight miles. Anyway, get rid of it.

ELLIS PARKER BUTLER TALKS ON HUMOR

Once upon a time (in the year 1905, to be exact) a gentleman named Ellis Parker Butler sent a humorous piece to Ellery Sedgwick, then editor of *Leslie's Monthly*. Mr. Sedgwick read the bit, changed its title from "The Dago Pig Episode" to "Pigs Is Pigs" and sent the gentleman named Ellis Parker Butler a check for $75. Following the publication of "Pigs Is Pigs," Mr. Butler's reputation was inaugurated, and the humorist gave up his editorship of and his partnership in the Decorative Furnisher, a magazine.

For the first time in his life, Ellis Parker Butler became a solicited author. He is still in that category. Incidentally, there are those who rank him in a class with Mark Twain, who, by the way, is Mr. Butler's favorite humorist.

Be that as it may, let us get to E.P.B.'s opinions of humor. They are exceedingly significant, and as such, are highly interesting.

"A 'sense of humor' and the art of creating humor are entirely different things," said Mr. Butler to me in his Flushing (Long Island) home. "They may be absolutely unrelated. The often-mentioned 'sense of humor' is merely incidental in the one who creates humor. The most successful humorist may not have it at all. If he has a 'sense of humor' in the beginning he is apt to lose it as he progresses, because he soon learns that the best humor is the result of an artful presentation of a subject rather than the result of any innately humorous quality of the subject."

"You mean that a professional humorist need have no sense of humor?"

"Exactly that. The "sense of humor' is the ability to laugh at what others might find annoying — to 'see the fun in things.' Some humorists may begin writing humor because they 'see the fun in things,' but I doubt if many do. We begin writing humor because we feel in ourselves — or discover in ourselves — the ability to make others see the fun in things. A master musician need not enjoy music; he must know how to write music others will enjoy or find interesting. A humorist need not enjoy humor; he must know how to make others laugh. Now, as the humorist progresses — learns his art — he discovers that it is an art. By building situation upon situation in certain ways, or by building word upon word in certain ways, he can, he finds, create a laugh producer. It becomes a serious matter with him, this trying to create the best humor he can. He has no time to bother with a 'sense of humor.' In his desire to be a great artist he may lose his 'sense of humor' entirely. The great humorist seldom laughs; he is serious. He knows the entire mechanism of humor so well that his 'sense of humor' becomes an ability to analyze; he is as little liable to laugh at funny things as a maker of fireworks is liable to exclaim when seeing a skyrocket explode. His thought is 'a good piece of work' or 'not so good!'"

"What is humor?" I asked, rather meekly, knowing that the question would be a sticker, especially to this humorist whom I had just obliged to forfeit an afternoon's nap.

Mr. Butler deliberated. "There are different answers to that," he finally replied. "Any number of definitions may be fitted to that query. Well, I should say that humor is any written or pictorial art that causes laughter. An excellent example of what is humorous in my opinion is Mark Twain's Jumping Frog. You ask me what is wit? Well, I should say that wit is mental brilliance. Wit may be natural. Humor is artificial. Humor must be wrought. It is the result of deliberation. But remember that there is that great difference between a 'sense of humor' and the actual humor. Humor must be treated by the writer before it can really be humor. Eli Perkins said that humor, in order to be considered as such, must first have the mark of the writer put upon it."

This brought me to the observation, "A humorist is born, not made." And so I inquired, "Do you believe that ability to be a humorist is born with a writer, or developed, or both, or either?"

"I have a pretty definite opinion about the matter. I believe that the real, the genuine humorist is born with the gift," answered Mr. Butler. "However, let it not be said that humor cannot be developed in a writer. It can be developed in almost anyone. Take a runner. He is usually the product of training. The same with the musician. He may have the talent, but he must be schooled in his art. And the same with the writer who is desirous of writing humor. Undoubtedly the genius is a born creature; nevertheless, one can be so trained that one's brain will function along the lines of humor."

Mr. Butler is of the belief that the best medium for the humorist today is the short story. "There is a bigger market for the humorous story," went on the leading American wit. "The narrative form is always the most popular form and for humor it is a natural vehicle. It is most effective. I don't doubt, however, that the essay will again come into vogue. It's bound to come in for its rightful share in the field of literature. As for the market for humor, it is quite extensive. There are plenty of magazines of all kinds that publish all kinds of humor. And most of them pay pretty good prices, too."

"What advice have you to give to would-be humorists?" I asked, bearing in mind the readers of *The Writer's Digest* who aspire to heights of humor.

"I'll tell you frankly," began Mr. Butler, "that I would not hesitate to advise my son to become a humorous writer. I think it is a good profession. You can and may work anywhere. Humor is easy to sell. The product is not bulky. The market is wide. Of course, it is easier for a writer when he lives in New York. Then he can query the magazines in this city on timely humorous material. A writer in California cannot very well query a New York magazine concerning material that must be written promptly and published shortly. And as much humorous material is written about current events, it therefore must necessarily be printed before the event has ceased to be current. You know some magazines have special numbers — automobile numbers, Gerald Chapman numbers, police numbers, and the like. Suppose that one of these magazines suddenly discovers that it hasn't sufficient Gerald Chapman material to build an issue with, what is that magazine going to do? Write to a humorist out in California? Hardly. It will notify a New Yorker promptly, who will be obliged to turn the stuff out presently. But let me give the beginner one good tip. Let him develop a distinct and distinctive personality in his humorous work. As examples of distinct personalities, let me cite Will Rogers, or George Ade. The writer mustn't change his personality either. He wants to have his readers get accustomed to his one particular aspect. In that manner, the humorist who has established a personality can be solicited by a magazine that is aware of the public's like for this peculiar personality. You readily see that today much of the humorous material appearing in print is monotonously alike. There is no individuality in much of it. The humorist who wishes to impress himself upon his audience must put something in that audience's head that it won't forget. And that is his own striking personality."

"Tell me something about this originality complex," I demanded, as if I were King.

"I'll say this about those who are too original when they start," continued Mr. Butler. "It seems that too many of them flop in a short time. These overly original youngsters who blossom forth of a sudden seem to peter out just as suddenly. It is advisable to choose some great humorist for your master, to start with. Strange to say, the apparent imitator, if he has talent, presently passes the one he has imitated, because his master is by that time a back number, while his ostensible imitator carries on into a new period, I don't mean that one must slavishly imitate someone else, but all the great humorists are representative types — the mock-egotistical, the mock-humble, the exaggerative, the playful, and so on — and the beginner should choose one as his model, and adhere to that type until his own personality emerges. You'll find that a great many writers who started by selecting some master as their model wound up by being supremely original themselves. You'll do best by adhering a little to the kind of humor that was successful before you. To try to be extremely original at the beginning is precarious. It creates small audiences, select perhaps, but never very faithful."

"You have doubtless heard of Professor Albert Gray Shaw of New York University," I began, "who recently declared that laughter is going to die out in time, especially when we become more sophisticated, and when incongruity, one of the elements of humor, is wiped out. What have you to say about that?"

Mr. Butler was definite in his opinions. "He's talking through his hat," he replied, in allusion to Prof. Shaw. "The more sophisticated a man becomes, the finer is his ability to appreciate humor. But we are not becoming sophisticated to any such extent as you imply. There is a small group of sophisticates, just as always, but the humorist can safely ignore it, unless he wishes to make it a subject of jest. The great mass of humanity is no more sophisticated than in the day of Pharaoh or the day of Lincoln. Humor is as necessary to people as food is. As a matter of fact, isn't it true that there never was a time when humor on the stage, in newspapers, in magazines, in speeches and in books was as greatly popular as it is today? The great mass of humanity does not vary one-tenth of one per cent in sophistication from age to age. The humorist today has larger audiences and is better remunerated than ever before; there are more people."

Inasmuch as this interview must be finished in 200 additional words, let me quote the major points of Mr. Butler's observations:

"The way in which a piece of humor is written is ninety per cent of the work," he went on. "Humor and profound writings get about the same, financially speaking. The syndication of humor is a great field. For the unknown, however, there is very little chance. A newspaper wouldn't take the trouble of looking at the work of someone it hasn't heard about, especially when it has to feature the writer. But the syndicate line is going to be bigger and bigger. Don't let the beginner be discouraged in the face of reputation. A big humorist, no matter how good and prolific he is, finds it pretty difficult to turn out a good piece each week. It's a real stunt to write humor to order. Another thing for the beginner to remember: Let him not be afraid to send his material to the better magazines. Suppose he submits excellent humor to the trashy, low-brow publication. They refuse him because he is simply too good for them. It's a serious mistake to be afraid of your market. Finally, let your readers know that it's preferable to write humor than serious stuff. That's how I feel about it. The humorist is always happy when he can turn out a splendid piece of work, and, incidentally, he makes someone else happy in turn."

TEN RULES FOR HUMOR

1

The first Method of Humor is what I might call a breezy exaggeration. It predominates in American humor. It is an inflated chest expansion. You take something only slightly important and permit it to grow, to wax large, until it is extremely important. A slight variation from the normal, aggrandized, enlarged tremendously, is a sure-fire success. Mark Twain was fond of this style. I used it in my article "Movies Is Movies" in *Photoplay* for July.

2

Second, we have the use of the other person's real or pretended ignorance. Almost all child humor is founded upon the child's ignorance of something we fully understand. International and rural humor of various kinds emanate from this. Wrong use of words, or, even to go further, another person's faults or peculiarities, may be classed here.

3

Third is what I call the naive mode, which Barrie so often employed in his early Scotch stories. By that I mean a seriousness, an alertness, about something that is really impossible, absurd or ridiculous. For example, I read a story just the other day about a postage stamp society which, at a meeting called to deplore the unornamental designs of postage stamps, appointed a committee to do away with the plain stamp now in use in the United States and persuade the government to issue a series of stamps displaying the scenery of California. That is the height of naive humor.

4

Fourth is the ridiculous, the calling direct attention to something we consider impossible in connection with ourselves — the fat man, in the silk hat, on a slippery pavement for instance. This is probably not funny to fat men in silk hats on slippery pavements.

5

Fifth, the repetition of something more or less unexpected. "Pigs is Pigs" is a good illustration of this. It starts as a sane story about an express company, an express man and a pair of expressed guinea pigs. Due to the well known rapidity of guinea pigs in multiplying, every time the express man comes around there are a few more pigs. Then there are a lot more. Each time, it's funnier. This is what I call beating upon the drum of humor.

6

Sixth is the sudden let-down from the extremely serious to the extremely frivolous. Mark Twain uses this where he is describing a young man who receives a severe calling down. The arraignment is noble, serious, solemn. But when he described the young man, he says he reminded him of a spider dropped on a hot skillet. First, a look of wild surprise, then he shrivelled.

7

The sixth example likewise explains the seventh method, the use of extreme analogy, calling attention to an agreement or likeness between things in some circumstances or effects when the things are otherwise entirely different. This is the basis of many cartoons.

8

The eighth is the more or less disguised practical joke, horse play, physical humor — the custard pie in the face. Strangely enough, if this is led up to in the right way, it is not raw or coarse, but is apt to be more effective than any other form of humor.

9

Ninth is the gradual expansion of an idea that has ridiculous possibilities, on the theory that if a little of a good thing is good, more is better.

10

The tenth is intempestivity, untimeliness, something that has no particular humor in itself happening at an opportune time — *mal apropos* humor. For example, things happening at a funeral, a wedding, a christening, or a gathering of a serious nature.

* * * *

Of course, it is understood that the author and the reader set themselves up as a superior set of persons. Humor is always laughing at something, and the author must convey the impression that he and the reader are laughing together at something.

Characterization is not humor. Characterization is the setting for humor. The better the setting, the more effective the humor. The contrast of action is more sharply defined. Things are often funny because of the character of the person who does them.

The after dinner speaker who starts out by saying 'Mike and Pat were walking down the street one day' is the bunk. Everybody at the table knows instantly that he has taken a stock setting — or no setting — for some words. There is no humor.

The great American novel? A myth — a symbol —an impossibility. None can write *the* great American novel any more than he can describe the spectrum in one word.

THIS FUNNY BUSINESS

Just for fun let us admit that I am in the humor-writing business. How did I get there? What happened? What can it suggest to another writer? Is it a good business? Is $13,600 a year a good income?

I began to write humor about 48 years ago, when I was in the Seventh Grade and twelve years old. On the top shelf of the school-room was a swishy raw-hide whip. My chum was a boy of my age and we were both bad little boys in school. The teacher had two favorite punishments for bad little boys — one was to keep them after school and swish their legs; the other was to make them write 300-word essays and read them before the school the next morning. My chum could not have written a 300-word essay in ten years, and reading it before a class would have been dire agony for him; I hated to have my legs swished — and never did have them swished.

The first time this teacher caught me in disobedience, she happened to fine me a 300-word essay. I wrote one on "Trees" in about six minutes, and it must have been humorous, for when I read it the teacher laughed and I laughed and the class laughed. After that I was punished often and I was considered a funny fellow. My chum continued to be swished. I knew then that humor was a fine business to be in.

In 1883, when I was 13, I sold my first humorous story to *Dawn of Day*, a boy's paper of Chicago, for fifty cents, which was paid me in one-cent post cards. This was the first money I had ever earned, and full grown men, working ten hours a day in the sawmills, got eighty cents a day, and were laid off all winter. My second story was bought for fifty cents by the same paper, but paid in cash.

From then on my life's work has been writing humor. In my early days I held many jobs as clerk, salesman, editor, but they were only to keep me alive while I wrote humor, and in 1906 I was able to give up all other jobs and be a professional humorist.

From the beginning I read all the humorous publications I could find — periodicals and books. I did have adaptability, which is a classy form of imitation. Adaptability is a most necessary quality for those who write to sell. Humor is merely the ability to tell a thing in a laughable manner, but it is not to be acquired; it is either born in a man or implanted in him at a very early age. You can't "make" a humorist, but more of us have the undeveloped seed of humor than is commonly supposed.

I saw at once that humor, in order to be readily salable, must be put in the form that is fashionable at the moment; this form is learned by watching the periodicals and the successful books of humor. You certainly do not want to use an Addisonian essay form if you hope to sell to Judge.

The best market is always the largest market, because there are more competitors for your product; I saw that the largest market was for fiction stories of 4,000 to 6,000 words; consequently I did — and have done — most of my humor in fiction form and that length.

You will notice, if you study the work of the successful humorists of today, that they fall into two rather distinct classes. In one class — as to form — are such admirable men as Robert Benchley, Stephen Leacock, and Will Rogers; in the other the equally admirable Octavus Roy Cohen, Clarence Buddington Kelland, and P. G. Wodehouse. The first write almost no plot fiction; the second put most of their humor into story form. Mark Twain was practically the first American professional humorist to use the story form; before him the professional humorist confined himself to the skit or short essay form almost exclusively. Benchley, Leacock, Rogers, etc., are the offspring of the pre-Twain humorists; Cohen, Kelland, Wodehouse, etc., date from Twain.

Both these forms of humor are legitimate and they have one common basic element, the most important in humor writing after an ability to get laughs is granted. This important thing is the ability to create and develop character, so that from the created character the laughable context is inevitable.

Cohen, for example, creates and develops Florian Slappey; Kelland creates Scattergood Baines; Wodehouse creates Jeeves. What Benchley creates as a character we all know? He creates Benchley. Will Rogers creates Will Rogers. Benchley, to those who read him, and Will Rogers, to those who hear or read him, are as much created characters in fiction as are Jeeves or Huck Finn. Midway between these two classes stands, for instance, P. Finley Dunne with his Mr. Dooley. Will Rogers is Will Rogers, but Dunne is Dooley and yet not Dooley, and Wodehouse is not at all Jeeves.

Gradually, if you continue to study the humorists, you will see more and more clearly that, whatever the type of humor or the form into which it is put, the development of character is the most important matter for the humorist. The little building of which Chic Sale wrote, is not very funny in itself; it might supply material for a one-minute joke to tell after half a dozen drinks at a club. But Chic Sale created a character and in the little book it is the Specialist who is funny — he is so serious; he is real; he is a genuine American character. We laugh because he is so confoundedly serious about a matter that is serious to him but laughable to us. Chic Sale's "Specialist" is as veritable a portrait as Rupert Hughes' Washington.

So we find that the real humorist — the important one — must concern himself with character creation. Bill Nye creates Bill Nye — the serious bald-headed jester; George Ade creates Artie and Doc Home; Townsend creates Chimmie Fadden; Bob Benchley creates Bob Benchley — the mock-serious, mock-eager, mock-erudite. Always it is the character-story or the character-man who is the great humorist.

Humor always creates a picture, and a properly developed character is more easily seen by the mind than one that is poorly and mistily sketched. We "see" Ring Lardner in his plotless skits because he develops a Ring Lardner character as he writes; we delight in Ring Lardner's plotted stories because he develops the characters in his stories so admirably.

You will find that when you think of the successful humorists, you think instantly of some important individual characteristic, in connection with each: Ade — slang, Benchley — mock seriousness; Frank Sullivan — extravagant burlesque; Will Rogers — philosophy, with a chuckle. The humorist who is not going to write fictional humor stories should develop an individuality of his own, for he is the "character" his audience sees. The humorist who is going to write fiction humor stories should give his greatest effort to perfecting his ability to create character. The best humor in fiction story humor does not lie in the plot; it results from the handling of a clearly-pictured character or two; in other words, the most successful humor is that which arises incidentally during the telling of the story.

When I have deviated from the above rules I have been unsuccessful; when I have stuck to them my writings have sold well. Leaving out motion-picture sales, book royalties, and other side issues, my income from humor was about $9,500 per year from 1906 to 1918. For some unknown reason it took a jump in 1919 and from 1919 to 1929 it has averaged about $13,600 a year. This included a couple of seasons of lecturing, but I found that platform work cut down my writing income just about as much as I took in from lecturing. During this period from 1919 to 1929 my lowest year was $9,300 and the highest $21,000.

I have an idea that if I had devoted my talent, such as it is, to the writing of non-humorous fiction I would have made a great deal more money — but I wanted to write humor. Humor, I think, loses out in comparison with serious fiction or other serious writing when it comes to book publication. Almost never does a humor book sell greatly; humor, as a rule, does not command a motion-picture sale. But there is the "Specialist" selling a million copies, I hear, and Ade and Rogers and Tarkington have done well with picture contracts. It is a gamble, I suppose.

My advice to one and all would be "If you like to write humor, go ahead and write it, but if you don't feel an eager impulse to make people laugh, don't bother with it." None of the very successful humorists are made; they were born.

Finally, humor is the easiest to test of any sort of writing. If you read a poem to a friend, or a group of friends, they may be doubtful; if you read a serious fiction story to them, they will hem and haw and say one thing and another; but if you read humor to any group and do not get a real laugh from some one, you can be mighty sure you haven't written humor.

Getting the laugh is the one and only test for humor. But not getting a laugh need not discourage you. If you get a grin you have got a sure seller. And anything that doesn't bring actual tears and sobs of woe is worth trying on an editor, poor long-suffering fellow that he is. I've never met an editor yet who did not say he needed more humor than he could get.

HOW I SELL MY STORIES

It is delightful to send out a manuscript and have it accepted by the first publication to which it is sent. This does happen now and then but it cannot happen always. It does not happen with me. If I write four stories each month and the first on my own market list is a monthly, I must inevitably get back at least thirty-six stories from that magazine, and I may get the whole forty-eight back. Then I have to send the manuscripts out again.

My "A" list has twenty magazines on it. I have sold to all these magazines, and to some of them many times, and they include all those that pay the best prices and are apt to use my stories.

My "B" list has twenty-nine magazines on it, and they are those that have bought at least one story from me but which pay lower prices. My "Occasional" list has nineteen magazines, and these are the magazines that are not in the market for my usual short stories but which do buy special articles occasionally, such as *Writer's Digest*, *Young Men*, *Printers' Ink*, and so on. I have also a "Short Humor" list, of periodicals that buy short humorous material, a "Juvenile List" for boy and girl stories, and a "Syndicate" list of the syndicates that buy short stories, either new or published. On all these lists I have the latest addresses and the names of the editors, and any other vital information. I use a card system for these lists.

But it will be seen that Lists "A" and "B" contain all the most likely markets for my short stories. The periodicals listed have either bought something from me, or have published stories similar to those I write.

On the tops of my bookshelves I have piles of all these "A" and "B" magazines, usually only one copy of each. Once a year, at least, I buy a new copy of each of the magazines. Sometimes I make the change much oftener. It is a good thing to keep a "library" of this sort and to take down, now and then, one of the magazines and study its contents. It keeps a man alive to what his markets are using.

The practical writer, by which I mean the man who wants to sell what he writes, should not be satisfied to know merely the name and general type of story wanted by a magazine. He should have a copy of the magazine and read it. He should come to know, in time, all the magazines on his lists, and there is no other way to do it. I read practically all the magazines on my "A" list every month or every week.

Now, suppose your story comes back from the first magazine to which you have sent it. That means almost nothing at all. The old phrase of the rejection blank "Return of the manuscript does not necessarily imply lack of merit" is absolutely true. You may have sent a golf story to a magazine that is already overloaded with golf stories. There are forty legitimate reasons why a magazine must decline a perfectly good story.

Quite often, however, something is wrong with the story itself, either for that particular magazine or for all magazines. Soon the manuscript, having been sent out again and again, begins to look shabby. The edges of the sheets get rough, the pages show their age. The manuscript shows that it has been sent around to many magazines.

I do not believe that many editors will reject a story because it shows this evidence of much travel, but there is a very good chance that a manuscript that has got into this condition has something the matter with it. The fact that it is frayed shows that it has been read — and usually hopefully — even by editors who received it when it was already shopworn.

I find that most of my manuscripts deserve retyping when they have been out from five to eight times, and I then either retype them myself or have them retyped. Sometimes I retype a story when it is returned the first time, and — as Chic Sale's Specialist says — I'll tell you why. It needs to be rewritten.

The chance is that when a manuscript of a story has been returned to the writer five or eight times it will be returned twenty more times because there is something wrong with it.

The writer most certainly has sent it the first few times to the editors most likely to accept it. Its chances of sale grow less with each additional sending.

That is the time to read the story — or article — and see what is the matter with it. Something is sure to be. So true is this that I told an editor the other day that most of my stories were not "written" but "rewritten." It is often the second or third writing of a story that sells it.

Mighty few writers are able to turn out perfect stories all the time at the first writing. Even when stories are revised many times at the first writing they are seldom all they should be, and for a very good reason. Story ideas or story plots usually snap into the writer's mind in a sort of red-hot glow. Even the writer with the lowest sort of enthusiasm greets his new plot or idea with a certain amount of pleasure. He sees a story in it. He thinks it over, arranges his characters, plans his introduction and the development of the story, and his climax for the end.

What happens? Often he loses much that he saw in the first glow. He may have thought of a character that would be delightfully quaint, but in working out the story with its many details the character becomes stale and flat. The writer may not know this — he still has the glow of the original thought with him — and the story is half on paper and half still in his mind. He can't help seeing it through rosy spectacles. Even if he half doubts that it is what he meant to write he hopes the editor will think it is great stuff.

The manuscript is sent out and it comes back. It is sent out several times more and it comes back. (Or it may be sent to an agent who gets it back again and again in the same way).

The point I want to make is that when a manuscript gets soiled it should be not only retyped but rewritten. Nine times out of ten a soiled manuscript is a warning that it should be rewritten. Read your soiled story again and you will see at once many things that are wrong with it. Your glow of creation is now gone, you can see the story as it is and as the editors saw it, and I'll warrant that you will be eager to change it in many places. Many times you will say, "Well, I don't won-der no editor wanted this!" I'll warrant, too, that you will have a better chance of selling the story after it is rewritten than you had in the beginning. In other words a "rejected" story has an equally good chance of selling as has a brand new one. It only needs rewriting.

There is another reason for rewriting a story after it has been circulated a number of times. The first lot of magazines to which you sent it usually exhausts the list of magazines apt to want the story as you have written it. Rewriting it with the next four or five magazines on your list in mind is sure to make the sale to one of them more possible.

But what you are able to do to the story in rewriting it is the most important matter. I had one recently that I had written in 1,800 words, hoping to sell it to some magazine on my "Short Humor" list. It was returned until it was soiled enough to retype, and when I read it over I found that the fun I had meant to put into the story was lost because I had not given the characters sufficient background. It could not be done in 1,800 words. I rewrote the idea into 5,000 words, using the same situation and characters, and sold it the next time I sent it out. More often I cut 6,500 words to 4,000.

Rereading the soiled pages is especially useful. Often the entire middle portion of my story remains clean when re-turned, with the first three or four and last two or three pages much soiled by handling. The editor or his reader has han-dled only these pages and has read only these pages, and has not read the part of the story where your best work is.

I can't object to this. The editor — and his reader — are experts and can judge a story by that much reading. They read the story to see whether their subscribers would like it, and neither you nor I like a story that has a long and tiresome beginning or a stupid and ineffective ending.

That may not be the trouble with any particular story, but it is very apt to be. Too often we take too long to get into our story, waste several pages in discursive descriptive writing that can be just as well left out or cut to half a page. I wrote a full half of my novel "The Jack-Knife Man" — ten chapters — and then began the novel with the tenth chapter, discarding the first nine as mere waste paper. You can write a thousand words describing a town, the scenery, what had happened, who the girl was and so on, and then improve the story by discarding 993 words and beginning with "Jane, blithe creature, ran down the walk."

When a story soils after a few sendings get at it and shorten the introductory pages. Nearly all stories are too long anyway.

Then — and you can usually do it while retyping — make such changes as hit your eye or mind while you are reading the middle portion of the story. If that part of the story disgusts you it would probably disgust an editor too, but if you see good in it the story is well worth rewriting. Cut anything that seems unimportant and unnecessary for the progress of the story. Watch the dialogue carefully.

Unless the title is an especially good one it is best to give the story a new title. With a new title and with the story rewritten you will send it out with greater confidence.

In rewriting never forget that you have exhausted a part of your list of magazines. Let the new title and the new introductory paragraphs be, as nearly as possible, what would appeal to the next six or eight magazines on your list. This is not bad art and it is good sense. And then consider seriously the last two or three pages of your story.

The end of your story should be a climax. It may be a few words spoken by one of the characters. It is worthwhile rewriting the last two pages of almost every manuscript every time it is returned. In the heat of writing a story the ending of it is far too often slurred. Does not the fact that the editor usually turns to the final pages show clearly that a first class ending might mean a story sold? The editor reads the first few pages and is not sure about accepting or rejecting; he turns to the final pages and then — rejects the story. Soiled final pages in a story manuscript mean that the story had a chance and lost it.

And, finally, this matter of rewriting a story when it needs retyping will soon lead to greater care in writing stories in the first place. Personally I almost never destroy a story — I rewrite it. Almost every story I have ever written has found a market sooner or later. But often the first form would not know the last form if they met on an editor's desk.

AN AUTHOR GLARES
AT EDITORS

All editors are numskulls part of the time, some editors are numskulls all of the time, and the majority of editors are numskulls most of the time.

That paraphrase may seem like wisecracking thunder to startle and challenge the attention, but it is a weighed, considered, literal and serious statement of opinion based on twenty-five years of professional contact with editors. If there is some rancor in the utterance, I hope to prove that it does not affect its essential verity.

That I broadcast from the privacy of *The Bookman* studio, instead of appearing in my own proper person, may impress you as discretion, cowardice, modesty or what you like. I think my reasons for anonymity are adequate, but whether they are or not doesn't affect the validity of the evidence. To coin a phrase, the facts speak for themselves.

But to spike possible discrediting of my testimony, I will offer this bit of negative information; my failure to identify myself is not due to failure in my profession. Periodically speaking (speaking of periodicals), I am a moderate success. I have also published a dozen books — none at my own expense. I have been syndicated and featured in newspapers. I am in *Who's Who*. I sell 98% of my stuff at prices good enough to earn me a quarter-century average of better than ten thousand a year. Which means that while I am not a "big name" I *am* an established author — or, if you prefer, a competent hack.

The Editor (who said he didn't mind being called a numskull, thus weakening my opening statement) will testify that I am not without honor in my own country.

I produce these few exhibits only to show that I'm not a "flop" blaming his own incapacity and futility on unsympathetic editors.

Why then bite the hands that feed me? I don't. The hands

that feed me are my own, pounding a typewriter, and pounding stamps on to fresh envelopes for remailing rejected manuscripts. Editorial hands for twenty-five years have been hands that metaphorically pushed me on the chest, poked me in the eye, clouted me on the chin and proved to be the hands that feed me only when my persistence and my ability to take punishment wrested a check from their weary fingers. I have a public and it likes my stuff — but the hammering I've had to do on editorial numskulls to break through to that public would erect a half-dozen skyscrapers.

I would write this rather in pity than in anger were editorial numskullity purely negative. Were they merely unresponsible to stimuli less delicate than the reiterated thump of a flat-wheeled trolley. But there is a form of numskullosity which is active, and which attacks the otherwise best of fellows the moment he sits behind an editorial desk. It's something like getting behind the steering wheel of a car. And you know what *that* does to manners.

Could I write a book!

Editors who send out word to aspiring young writers that they are too busy to see them — their busyness consisting of a crap game! Editors who *ask* you to send in stuff and then return it with a rejection slip — and often without even that printed regret. Editors of a new magazine, starving for material, trying to get first-rate stuff for third-rate prices — returning with a rejection slip, a well-known author's manuscript (not mine) which had been submitted with a pleasant personal note. Editors who go "third person" on their intimate friends and have their secretaries write "Mr. Numskull is sorry, but —" instead of "Dear Bill: This stuff won't do." Editors who send out word to regular contributors to wait a little, and then after forty-five minutes tell the girl outside to say that Mr. Numskull is, after all, too occupied to grant an interview. Editors who fall on your neck at the Club and rave over a contribution you have sent them, saying it's what they've wanted for eons — and send it back two days later with no explanation, and no attention whatever to your subsequent "How-comes?" Editors who tell you they will be in the office until twelve o'clock and will be glad to see you — and then go out to lunch at 11.30 with no apology or excuse left behind to compensate for your forty-mile trip from Suburbia. Editors who write you to come in and discuss a proposed feature — their proposal — and keep you standing in a chairless cubby-hole of a "reception room" while they talk to you. (That one, however, was O. K. by me — in resentment I doubled the price, and got it.)

These are not just casual discourtesies, they are constant — like bad manners in the driver's seat. But far more unintelligent than motor-rudeness, which is directed at total strangers, while editorial bad manners slap the faces of those who make the magazines — which is bad business. As anybody but a numskull would know.

"But authors are a sensitive race — they make too much of these things." If authors really were a sensitive race they'd have been extinct long ago. But assume they are sensitive, wouldn't it be politic to smooth their antennae instead of breaking them off?

"Editors are very busy people, they can't see everybody." I don't know whether there is a word called "hooey" in the dictionary, but I know there is one called "buncombe."

Let me quote the late and beloved Fat Bill Johnstone, sometime Sunday Editor of the *New York World* in its days of greatest power and prosperity, and author of the Limpy stories of considerable renown a decade ago.

Said Bill: "An editor who is too busy to see any and everybody who may have something on the ball is falling down on his job. If seeing ninety-nine would-be writers and artists is a waste of time, the hundredth leaves you with a profit. I see 'em all — and I do my other work too without undue strain. Any fool can keep the wrong people out of his paper, my job is to get the right ones in."

He got them, too. The list of those he gave a start is pretty near the table of contents of any magazine that specializes in big names. Furthermore, so long as Bill held down that chair he could have the best from any of those big names — at space rates. For authors are grateful. If Bill had time to be courteous, so have other editors.

But there is a much more serious charge against editorial ethics. And one to which authors never become inured, because it violates ordinary business rules. *The average editor does not keep his word.* True, he seldom gives it — wangling speculative stuff out of authors with no definite agreement being regarded as brilliant editorial achievement. But when he does give it, you can't count on it.

In the writing trade I'm known as a dependable performer. Yet, time after time, after definite verbal agreement that if a scenario was satisfactory the material would be considered as on order — I have had the final stuff turned down. And never on the ground that the work itself wasn't my usual. Always with the regretful explanation that the ideas didn't seem so good as on their submission, or the material wasn't timely, now (though delivered when ordered). "You could sue me."

Once, at the suggestion of one of the editorial prima donnas, I did some stuff as outlined by *him* for his particular magazine for that immediate time. It would have no market elsewhere. Two weeks later it was returned with the information that Mr. Numskull had decided his own idea wasn't so hot, after all. And no offer to pay me even for my time.

Yet that editor wouldn't dream of telling his tailor he wanted a suit of a certain fabric, cut and style which nobody else could wear — and then reject and refuse to pay for the suit because he'd decided he didn't want that kind of suit after all. For tailors, unlike authors, are a sensitive race.

Lest these examples of numskullduggery might be considered personal peevishness I refer you to the files of the Authors' League or to Mr. William Hamilton Osborne, attorney for the League, and an author himself, for proofs of the prevalence of editorial instability in the spoken and the written word.

One of the most successful article writers in the country

— you'd know his name instantly if I used it, which I won't — said to me recently, "I've quit. I've been thrifty and I had a little luck in the market, too. I've an income of $7,500 a year and I'm satisfied. I made thirty to forty thousand a year out of article writing, but I'd rather have my seventy-five hundred and not have to deal with editorial so-and-sos any longer. They don't keep their word, they don't keep their contracts and their ethics — well, they ain't got no ethics. And no manners. I was treated better when I used to be a book agent than I have been in editorial offices."

Extreme and harsh language — but any freelance article writer will echo it.

However, bad manners and bad ethics, though numskullish in their ultimate effect, are not sufficient proofs of incompetence. Difficult as they make the author's already thorny way he might still respect the perpetrators if they were otherwise adequate to their jobs. But they aren't. Editors are numskulls in their judgment of the material they publish. Their magazines succeed — where they do succeed — in spite of them, not because of them. Of course this isn't 100% true, any more than most of my other accusations are 100% true. But it is more than 50% true, and what I'm proving is that my opening statement is sound and not mere fury.

If editors were not numskulls they ought to know approximately what they want for their magazines, and they ought to recognize it when they get it. Do they?

I have just been going over the record of my *sold and published* manuscripts for the past two years. I took them as they came — A to Z. Stories, sketches, articles, essays, novelettes — both commissioned material and purely speculative. I found that out of one hundred and twenty-five manuscripts, twelve had been to more than thirty markets apiece — and then sold. Of this twelve, *nine were sold to magazines which had formerly rejected them.* One was sold to a market that had rejected it three times. Three had been rejected twice by the final buyer. The *total* number of manuscripts sold to editors who had tossed them back at me at least once was eighteen. Two manuscripts had made forty-two trips each and sold on the third round to a former rejecter. Two had been to thirty-eight markets — and sold the second round. And one had been sold — and profitably — to the *seventy-fourth* market attacked. The *average* number of submissions of these manuscripts was just over ten.

At first glance this may seem proof that I am a numskull author not to know my market better. Why didn't I send this stuff to the last place in the first place? In eighteen instances I did *just* that — and was turned down. The rest of the answer is that editors are so uncertain of their judgment and so unpredictable in their sudden enthusiasms and equally mercurial antipathies that the first place your experience tells you to send a manuscript is just at that particular moment the last place you can sell it.

How can you figure them when an editor will turn down a story and then write you letters asking for "something like that" when the contribution appears somewhere else?

If it's their own ideas which govern them, why do they decline stuff on grounds of policy? If it's magazine policy that guides them, why will one editor be a steady buyer from a contributor, his successor never buy from that contributor, and *his* successor become a buyer again?

How can an author calculate on such a market?

Recently I made a laboratory test. I wrote ten manuscripts definitely designed for the particular policies, leanings, and prejudices of ten different periodicals.

Well, they're all sold now. *Not one of them to the original editor I selected.* Average number of submissions — nine. Should it take nine editors to make a man who knows his manuscripts?

If they know their business why was I four years in selling a certain manuscript which was bought by an editor who had turned it down three times — when its publication not only made a hit but altered the entire policy of the magazine? If they know their business why was my idea for a series of sketches pooh-poohed by an editor for three years — only to have him suggest such a series as his own idea at the end of the three years?

If they know their business why do they so often write "we had a rip-roaring time reading your story in this office, but we're afraid the average reader —"? If they didn't cultivate a superior attitude it might occur to them that if they had a rip-roaring time maybe the readers would too. If they know their business why did a friend of mine get back a manuscript from one of the editors of a magazine saying he was sorry but it was too highbrow for their readers, and get it back again a year later from another of that same staff saying he was sorry, but it was too lowbrow for their readers?

Once on a time I wrote a twenty-thousand word tale called *Adventure, Steady Boarder.* It began its travels, and continued them always accompanied by this brief note of explanation:

"Dear Mr. Numskull: The enclosed is a series of stories about the characters in a boarding house to show that the dullest of them have had their adventures. It must be considered wholly on its entertainment value and not as a conventional novelette." It went to twenty-six places before it landed. And at least half the editors informed me that my opus was "entertaining, but not a novelette."

After about the fifteenth rejection I happened to tell an editor of this experience. "I'd like to see that story," he said. "All right," sez I, "but remember it is a series of related incidents bound together only by the idea of adventure, and in no sense a conventional novelette." "That doesn't matter if it's sufficiently entertaining," he replied. "Let me read it."

Ripley me or not, ladies and gentlemen, he sent it back with this note: "Dear Anon: This is a nice thing you've done and enormously interesting, but you see it isn't a novelette and thus must go back to you."

(Oh yes, I sold it eventually — as a series of short stories!)

Once an editor wrote. "Dear Anon: — We're glad to take *Gobs of Gold* and check is enclosed. *Slews of Silver* which is also enclosed I think we have seen before."

My reply: "Dear Numskull: Thanks for the check. But why the pained surprise at seeing *Slews of Silver* again? You saw *Gobs of Gold* before, too — six months before you bought it!"

Once more let's shift from the particular to the general. I ask you to believe that I cite my own experiences only when they seem to me interesting illuminations of my general indictment.

Kenneth Roberts tells in the *Saturday Evening Post* how Tarkington's *Monsieur Beancaire* — one of the greatest if not *the* greatest romance ever written — was numskulled from one editor to another until Tarkington's sister fairly thrust it down the throat of the old *McClure's*. "The moron public", of which editors talk so much, knew it was great stuff the minute it appeared — any numskull but an editor can *feel* genius even if he can't pass a Binet test.

When one thinks of the immediate response of that same "moron public" to authors whom the editors take years to recognize, one is convinced that editors who try out stuff on the office boy and the telephone girl are guilty of the exercise of more than numskull intelligence.

You may think O. Henry was a great writer or a mere trickster — but he brought a fresh note into American literature and almost revolutionized the short story. Yet his early stories — and the early ones were among his best — got dog-eared traveling from big mag to big mag and were engulfed in the maw of the pulpwoods, which have to buy nearly everything that has plot and action to feed their presses. That's why editors of pulpwoods are always "discovering" authors. If they fill their mags they *have* to discover them. But they wouldn't have the chance if the "big" editors were as big as they're supposed to be, because every new author tries the big leagues first.

If editors weren't numskulls why did Joseph Hergesheimer have to wait twelve years for recognition — or even acceptance? Do you believe for one minute that everything he did in those twelve years was unworthy of publication?

If editors aren't numskulls why did Jack London have to struggle and starve for years to stir editors, when his stuff stirred the "moron public" the instant it began to appear? And if you believe none of his early stuff worth publication, read *Martin Eden* and learn how he sold it later at top Jack London prices. Did you know also that Jack — not when he was struggling, but when he had arrived — said that "Most editors are writers who have failed"?

Did you know that George Allan England, a first-rate craftsman if there ever was one, worked for ten or twelve years for the two-cent-a-word magazines before he had a glimmer of encouragement from the big mags? And that a cub reporter's story — which wasn't true — that England was going to quit writing in disgust and run a chicken farm — won him more offers from editors than all his honest work had ever accomplished?

Did you know that Sam Merwin, co-author with H. K. Webster of *Calumet K* which took the country by storm, and author thereafter of many successful short stories, was told, after but two years' absence from the writing field as an editor, "We don't know you. Go get a reputation."

He went and got it, all over again, and the same scornful editors paid him fat prices, while Sam smiled his benign smile.

Did you know that the late C. E. Van Loan — best of sports-story writers — Arthur Somers Roche, and Leonard Nason — among many, were pulpwood slaves for years before they got even a nibble from the high-and-mighties, and that not one author in twenty gets a break from the "big" editors who are "searching always for material", until he has pounded his fingers flat for the little mags and the daily short-story syndicates?

Of course an author must serve an apprenticeship — and God knows most of us do. But that apprenticeship is on the average at least four years longer than it would be if editors half knew their business, if they weren't numskulls, and sheep-minded ones at that. They wait for the other fellow to make a discovery, and the other fellow waits for them. They'd rather keep ninety-nine lambs out of the fold than let one in. They are afraid of the advertiser, afraid of the publisher, afraid of taking a chance, afraid of ideas, and afraid of the public which they despise. They lunch with each other for fear they might be contaminated by some of that public, and hence they know nothing about it. They huddle in conferences over stories for fear they might publish one that somebody would dislike.

Once in a while one of them inadvertently lets something different and unusual into his magazine — and it scores a success. Then he goes on trying to repeat that exact kind of success and all the others tail after him. An editor moves from one magazine to another — and duplicates number one.

They have more taboos than a South African savage. Taboos on sex, or taboos on anything but sex. Taboos on religion, politics and sociology. Taboos, in fact, on anything which elicits three indignant letters from a circulation of a million. And taboos on taboos which some rarely courageous editor has demonstrated ain't so.

If they were really competed they would hold their jobs. So far as I recall, there is just one editor of one nationally circulated magazine who still sits where he sat twenty-five years ago. A number of them are dead. Some of them have stepped to bigger editorial jobs — but not many. The mortality of jobs among editors is higher than in any profession or business with which I am familiar — including even actors.

This may prove that publishers are difficult to work for, but to me it proves that most editors fall down on their jobs. And we authors suffer because of the everlasting shifts in personalities and policies due to that incompetence. The public suffers, too, because originality, freshness and vitality have to break through so much editorial incapacity to reach the reader.

There are splendid exceptions- — but not many of them. There are editors whose courtesy and eagerness to give the beginner a chance are limitless. There are editors whose word is their bond — and it's a gilt-edged bond. There are editors with courage, initiative, imagination and true sensitiveness. And these noble exceptions are the manna in the author's desert. Without them we'd *all* be chicken farmers.

www.ingramcontent.com/pod-product-compliance
Lightning Source LLC
Chambersburg PA
CBHW030308030426
42337CB00012B/628